Hurting Hearts Need a Light

An inspirational read that offers hope and encouragement

Debbie Erickson

Cover Image: Samantha Fury, Cover@FuryCoverDesign

Editor: Maleah Bell

Printed in the United States of America

18 19 20 21 22 23—6 5 4 3 2 1

ISBN – 13 978-1987590029

ISBN – 10 1987590023

Dedication

This book is dedicated to all the hurting hearts in the world that wonder if they will ever see tomorrow.

There is hope. There is a light at the end of your tunnel.

Step back.

Take a deep breath.

Breathe.

This is a new beginning to the rest of your life...

Contents

Introduction

Imagine that you and I are sitting in a cozy living room with a fire ablaze in the fireplace and you're sipping your favorite beverage. I give you time to take in the ambience and then ask, "How are you doing?"

You respond, "Pretty good, I guess."

I nod and lift the corners of my mouth. "I mean, how are you *really* doing?" When I ask the second time, you realize that I'm serious and interested in how your life is going.

You sigh. The room is silent except for the crackling of the logs. You look out the window; snow is falling. As the candles on the mantle flicker, you realize that you need to talk. After a few minutes, you allow me to enter your world. You tell me how things are really going and how you've been feeling. You trust me enough to open the fountain of your heart and invite me in.

You tell me about your deepest hurts—the mountains you've climbed, the dark valleys you've descended, and the raging seas of unrest you may have experienced—depression, divorce, the death of a loved one, or children who have let you down. You look at me and realize that maybe, for the first time, someone really does care about your life . . .

In this inspirational booklet, I've compiled thirteen short Inspirational stories to encourage you not to give up; no matter how dire your circumstances; no matter how much your heart aches. You can be set free from your past if you don't give up.

I've gone through my share of valleys, and I couldn't see a light at the end because of the shadows that blocked my way. I know what it's like to struggle with depression and loneliness and how it feels when you believe no one cares about you or loves you. You may or may not have experienced the same things that I have, but what's important is how you're feeling right now and whether you want to work toward a solution.

My sincere desire is to briefly share some of my struggles that took me down long roads of despair, and I want you to know that it is possible to plant your feet on the mountaintop where God wants all of us to be because of His great love for us.

You can live a life of joy if you discover your God-given purpose. Once you do you'll be able to set your feet on a new journey that offers hope, one where you can walk through a door and find the joy Jesus offers. He has a plan for all of us, and He'll help you walk closer to Him. Life is an arena: choose to step inside and experience your purpose.

May you find comfort as He speaks to your heart and guides you to discover your true purpose so that you can begin working toward a goal.

~ In His Service ~ Debbie Erickson

1

Grace

My grace is sufficient for thee: for my strength is made perfect in weakness.—2 Cor. 12:9

I considered saving what I believe to be the most encouraging message in the Bible for last, but I realized that I need to open with it because it's one of the greatest gifts that God bestows on us . . . *Grace.*

The day that fear caused my world to go black gripped me as it wrapped its tentacles around me. It felt as though I was suffocating. I didn't know what was happening because I had never felt that way before. I thought I was dying.

Another day, years later, I became frightened when I felt abandoned. I had been through a sequence of setbacks that had nudged me to the foot of God's throne. I knew that it was just God and me. I cried out to the only One I knew could help me. I felt empty. Helpless.

When I think about those times, it seemed that in order for me to grasp the full meaning of His grace I had to go through those things. Those days had a profound effect on me: I had no other choice than to look up for help.

I had professed Jesus as my Lord and Savior, I had been baptized into Christ by immersion, and I wanted to put God first in my life, and so I did. But I endured some hardships along the way.

I had struggled with depression. Even when I was around other Christians, I always felt as if I was walking alone. It wasn't because they didn't *want* to help; it was because they didn't know *how* to help because depression wasn't something where there was a quick fix. So I'd keep things to myself, which was a mistake. You see, the enemy wants to isolate us from our family and friends. I began withdrawing and building a wall so no one could hurt me, which was the worst thing I could have done.

My struggles continued, but I strived to stay connected to God's Word. Since Psalms is a wonderful book for the brokenhearted, I read it frequently for comfort. I didn't know how to handle the things that were going on in my life, and I made my share of mistakes. Everyday seemed to be constant turmoil and chaos. My prayer life was constant because I always felt as though I was drowning in a sea of sorrow trying to keep my head above water. But God was faithful and with His help I overcame and continued to walk with Jesus with a sincere and fervent heart. *Grace.*

I had read many books on God's grace, but I had always struggled to understand its full potential. "I don't get it," I said; and the reasons were these: (1) it sounded too good to be true; and, (2) sadly, I lived a lot of my Christian life as if God had a merit-based system: the more good things I did, the happier He would be with me. I can't remember why I believed that, but I always felt that God wasn't very happy with me most of the time. *Guilt.*

Then my day of reckoning came when God in His mercy stepped in and helped me understand the full extent of His grace. I had imagined Him saying, "Okay, it's time for you to understand what My grace is all about." So He reached down and did something.

Fear is a very real emotion. I was full of fear and despair, but God didn't cause my fear; I caused my churning heart to fear because I allowed my emotions to run wild. I found myself in a position where I knew no one would be able to help me but God. *It's just me and you, God. No one else can rescue me. I need You. Only you can save me from me and others.* It was very intense and emotional.

I was at the foot of God's throne, just Him and me. I was shaky scared, but at that moment I realized He really was the only One who could help; and I knew I was doomed if He didn't.

God didn't forsake me. He didn't walk away. And even though it felt as if He was being silent, His grace and love do not flow because of how we *feel*. He reached down that night because of His unconditional love. He got my attention. The floodgates opened as He spoke to my heart, silently and tenderly. I could do nothing but listen in the dead silence. His kind and loving words washed over me, "My grace is sufficient for thee: for my strength is made perfect in weakness" (2 Cor. 12:9).

"What!" I had read this verse many times, but I felt it was for everyone but me. Even sadder, I had lived the majority of my Christian life that way. Then I began to wonder where my joy had been all those years, because I had none. Who can have joy when fear is all you know? I had faith and believed there was nothing God couldn't do because "with God all things are possible" (Matt. 19:26; Mark 10:27). I had lived a life that wasn't healthy; I had become physically, mentally, emotionally, and spiritually drained. How could I expect anything different?

After rising from the ashes of my fears that night, I realized that it was God's grace that I needed, not someone else's. I accepted His gifts of love, forgiveness, mercy, and grace. He cared enough to help me understand His grace.

Sometimes we don't understand the things of God; and when we don't, we can indeed "walk by faith, not by sight" (2 Cor. 5:7) because of Biblical truths. God brought me to the footstool of His throne so I could understand that His grace really was (and is) "sufficient" for me. My greatest regret is that it took me so long to realize it. Grace is like a *golden nugget . . . priceless.*

That's some of my story. What's yours?

For those who have never been able to understand God's grace, it is my sincere prayer that you will realize how important you are to God and that *His grace is sufficient for you, too,* no matter where you are in your life's journey or how you may be feeling. His love covers a multitude of sins. Don't go one more second without realizing the extent of His grace, even if you must wake up each morning and declare 2 Corinthians 12:9; "My grace is sufficient for thee."

When it's just you and God alone, I pray that you understand His grace and accept it. It's a free gift (Eph. 2:8). And while His grace doesn't give us permission to sin, when we belong to Him we are cleansed from all unrighteousness when we confess our sins to Him (1 John 1:9 NASB).

May you walk in the joy, peace, and grace of our Lord and Savior, Jesus Christ, as He intends for us to do, and may they overflow in your life. I hope you'll find encouragement wherever you are in your journey.

2

What's Your Passion?

"Seek ye first the kingdom of God, and His righteousness; and all these things shall be added unto you." — Matthew 6:33

I shared with you that I struggled with depression many years ago. It wasn't a temporary kind of depression. It was severe, and it lasted for months. I lost joy, and I lost hope. Life wasn't any fun. It felt as though I was hanging on to a thread that stretched down from the universe. I believed God was holding the other end of the thread, but I couldn't feel His presence. I felt alone in my struggles, and even antidepressants didn't help.

Then a friend gave me a book titled, *The Wall: A Parable* by Gloria Jay Evans. As I read this simple, childlike book, it sounded as though the book had been written just for me. It dealt with *the wall* that I had built around myself, stone by stone, until the wall was so high and thick that no one could possibly penetrate it—no one would ever hurt me again. That wall had become my *safety zone*: safe from a cruel world. But, in time, I grew lonely inside the wall, and it caused me to die emotionally. The wall did exactly the opposite of what I wanted. It was so dark, and I believed that life held no meaning or purpose. What was I really good for? Good at?

The book had simple illustrations, and the story captured a snapshot of my life. I had become a prisoner—paralyzed with fear—and it was the fear that urged me to tear down the wall. So, I pushed out a brick. Then another. Soon, Jesus' light shone inside and began to warm my face. He took my hand, and He helped me to begin tearing down the wall. It was hard at first because I didn't want to be vulnerable to the world, but I realized that it was better to be vulnerable and free than to hide in a dark and lonely place.

Sometimes we can shove our hurts so far down that it becomes a natural instinct to build a wall, and we strive to keep the wall in place. But is that really living? To be so

15

afraid of getting hurt that you remain paralyzed inside your own world?

When I realized the damage that wall had caused me, I knew I wanted out. God gave me the strength to remove the stones, one by one, until the wall fell. I was finally free to live, to love, and to take a chance on life again.

God also showed me how important it is to have people in your life who sincerely care enough about you and your situation that they want to help you tear down the wall so you can be restored. He taught me how important nutrition and exercise are when you're feeling depressed. But what I realized most that without purpose and meaning in your life, there is little hope for a brighter future on this earth.

That brings us to the point of this chapter.

Everyone is born with a purpose

Everyone is born with a purpose, even though many people may not know exactly what that purpose is. We're not just born, live, and then die without a purpose. If this were true, life would be meaningless, and we'd feel like insignificant beings walking blindly into an unknown future without hope. Finding purpose in my life gave me a breath of fresh air. It opened up a world that I had never experienced, and I know that finding your purpose and passion can do the same for you.

I had always loved to write. As the years passed, my desire grew, but my life didn't allow me to pursue my dream back then. I had to "give up" a hundred times, but my passion for writing wouldn't allow me to give up for good.

Wouldn't you like to discover your passion? Your purpose in life? I'd love to see you pursue your goals and dreams and use them for God's glory so you can give hope and encouragement to others.

The good news is that we're not just here taking up space. We each have a gift; something that we can do better than anything else, or anybody else. And that gift wants to be freed.

Maybe you need to further your education, hone your skills in a particular activity, take some lessons, or learn a new craft that you've always wanted to pursue and think you would enjoy, but you just never took the time to step out. Maybe you've already discovered your passion, but you don't know how or where to begin.

Teaching Sunday school or being a church leader? Graphic design? Writing? Gardening? Maybe you are interested in sewing children's clothes or doll clothes or making quilts? Woodworking, such as building birdhouses, flower boxes, planet stands, and so forth? Computer skills, building websites, or blogging? Social skills? Working with disabled children? The library has books on these subjects with many suggestions. Even with little to no experience, it's never too late to learn a new career, trade, or hobby.

What excites you? What activity makes you happy when you're participating in it? I'd like to challenge you to discover your passion by stepping out to discover God's purpose for your life. Here are five things that might help to move you toward that goal:

1. First, sincerely pray and ask God for His guidance. Take your time and think about what activity you would enjoy doing more than anything else.
2. Then, make a list. Write down as many things as you can think of that you would enjoy doing.
3. With your list, do some research, either on the Internet or at the library. Read up on what's involved with each item on your list to see if it is something you'd really enjoy. You may change your mind about an activity after you discover what's involved, and that could save you time and money.
4. Next, narrow your list. Pick the top three or four things that you think you would enjoy doing more than any others (and possibly make some extra money

at!) and something you believe you would be good at, and go for it! Educate yourself on the pros and cons, and stay focused on the things you think would have a chance of becoming a reality for you.

5. After pinpointing those things, pray again for God's guidance and direction. Seek His will and His plans for your life so that in the end, whatever you choose, you'll feel confident that He's behind you and able to sustain you through the ups and downs. Most importantly, go into it with an attitude of glorifying Him. Matthew 6:33 says, "Seek ye first the kingdom of God, and His righteousness; and all these things shall be added unto you."

Finally, be sure to seek out people who are willing and able to help you achieve your goal(s). By researching and asking questions, you'll gain much knowledge.

One of my passions is encouraging others through my writing, but it hasn't been an easy road. Perseverance is key. Is there something hindering you from achieving your goal(s)? Where does your true passion lie? ~ Blessings and happy discovering.

3

Reaching Your Dreams

*"'For I know the plans that I have for you,' declares the L*ORD*, 'plans for welfare and not for calamity to give you a future and a hope.'"—*
Jeremiah 29:11 NASB

I hope you've given some thought about what you would like to do with your life and where your interests lie. Maybe you would like to try some new things, but you feel overburdened with other priorities.

I've felt that way, too.

I read a post once about how people spend their time and how fast time goes. And it seems the older we get, the faster it goes.

"Time is money," as the saying goes, but time is also

precious. Many times we wish we had more hours in our days. Time management and straightening out our priorities isn't easy unless we begin to condition ourselves to put forth the effort toward that goal.

Do you struggle with time management? If you have a family, it may be harder to find time for yourself. So you must grab it when you can.

When my children were growing up, everyday was challenging and busy: running errands, taking them back and forth to sporting practices and events, attending school functions, and so on, but I never regretted those days.

I tried to write during those years; and while I did write some short stories, I never really had a chance to work on any kind of career. Though there were times when life was hectic, I felt blessed just to have the opportunity to watch my children grow—exactly what God had planned.

Things to Consider

Maybe the time isn't right for you to pursue any kind of career right now; If so, understand that you are right where God wants you to be, but that doesn't mean you can't *plan* on what you might enjoy doing in the future when the time presents itself.

First: Family

Maybe you're busy devoting your time and energy to your family, which is awesome. Nothing is wrong with that. In the meantime, possibly you can find some time to think about how you could use your talent(s) after your children are grown and leave the house.

Keep a journal. Prepare for the time when you'll be able to use your abilities for God's glory. For example, I'm gathering photos of my grandchildren to put them to a music video, and present it to them at their graduations. You may consider this as well. After you become a pro, maybe you would like to do this for other parents and earn some money in the process.

Second: The Elderly

I'm sure many elderly people would love someone to take an interest in them and help them with things they may find difficult: offering to pick something up at the store for them, or mowing their lawn, for example. If they're able to get out of the house, I'm sure they'd love to go to breakfast a few times a month or go to the mall for the opportunity to be around other people.

Ask them about their lives, and keep a journal. Encourage them to tell you their stories. The elderly love to reminisce and talk about their past. I'm sure they have some interesting stories to tell, and you just might hit on a nugget that you could use to help others. Take notes, and ask for permission to tell their stories so you may be able to publish an anthology or use the stories on your blog site.

Third: Children

Things can be a little sticky nowadays when it comes to kids, and we need to be careful how we approach children who belong to others. But if you have children of your own, I can almost safely assume that you're around a lot of other children their age. There is a treasure trove of funny and heartwarming things that kids say about *life*, *love*, and *families*! Ask them questions, and keep a journal. Kids will be honest with you. But if you decide to talk with children other than your own, be sure to seek permission from their parents, and talk to them with their parents present. It is also important to have their parent(s) sign a release form giving you permission to publish (or not).

Check out this site for inspiration: *"Money-making Hobbies for Women That'll Make You Pursue Them,"* at *https://hobbyzeal.com/money-making-hobbies-for-women.*

You can get lots of hobby and craft ideas on Pinterest.com for women and men.

I learned through a difficult situation how perfect God's timing is. He knows what's best for us, He understands our hectic schedules, and He loves and cares about what happens in our lives, big and small. He understands that life happens, but "all things work together for good to them that love God, to them who are the called according to his purpose" (Rom.8:28). Remember, He knows what's best, and His timing is perfect. Although we may not feel the same, we can't see the whole picture, so we need to trust Him to lead us down the path that He chooses for us. In the end, He asks to receive the glory. He wants us to enjoy life. He wants the best for us. And He wants us to exercise the talents He's given us. If we can discover what we really enjoy doing, it will bring joy and a sense of accomplishment to our lives.

"'For I know the plans that I have for you,' declares the LORD, 'plans for welfare and not for calamity to give you a future and a hope'" (Jer.29:11 NASB), *and.* . . "Finally, brethren, whatever is true, whatever is honorable, whatever is right, whatever is pure, whatever is lovely, whatever is of good repute, if there is any excellence and if anything worthy of praise, dwell on these things" (Phil.4:8 NASB).

Do you struggle with time management? Begin anew to take steps to help you reach your goals in the future. Persevere. Do your best to overcome the obstacles.

4

Who Are Your Friends?

Casting all your anxiety on Him, because He cares for you.—*1Peter 5:7 NASB*

Do you sometimes feel beaten down by the world? Do you spend your time around persons who say, "You can't," rather than those who tell you that you can?

It's easy to get swept up in other people's downers, and it seems that negativity is becoming the norm in our society. I've been around persons who constantly have drama in their lives—every day is a major crisis to them. They speak negatively and have very few positive things to say.

However, with that said, I've been there a time or two myself. So I can empathize because I know life can get hard.

Life is short; the older we get, the faster it passes. It's way too short to be negative, and it's too short to be around those who constantly bring us down—verbally and/or emotionally. But there is a flip side.

As we grow in God's love and grace, we realize that we really can live a less stressful life by doing our best to stay positive, even though that can be difficult at times. I've discovered that it takes more energy to be negative than it does to be positive. A negative attitude puts stress on our hearts and bodies. The Bible says we are to cast "all [our] anxieties on Him, because He cares for [us]" (1Pet.5:7 NASB). And God does care for us more than our finite minds can fathom.

If we must be around negative-thinking people, let's strive to be a witness for God and bring them up. When we look around on the world's stage, we can find plenty of people who are hurting, who feel lost and without hope. If we begin seeing them through the eyes of Christ, we can find opportunities to share Him with those who may not know Him personally.

I titled this chapter, "Who Are Your Friends?" because it doesn't take much for someone to bring us down. Are you rising above the negativity and negative voices in your life—voices that try to steal your hope, dreams, and joy and bring you down to a level where you don't want to go? Some voices will try to even steal our motivation to try. And whether we like it or not, whether we believe it or not, there will always be those voices that will try to harm us and bring us down to their level. Let's ignore their rhetoric and instead, let's be a light unto their path and lift them up to a more positive level.

What can we do to stay positive when society seems to be falling apart?

1. First and foremost, spend quality time around friends who truly love and care for you and who will provide encouragement—friends who want the best for you and who love to reinforce God's truths to help you rise above the negativity.

2. Don't look at the world's standards to gauge your life. Don't look for hope or encouragement from the world and worldly minded people; you won't find it there.

3. Finally, and most importantly, read encouraging books and articles by *successful, godly people* who can help you in your journey and who have walked down the same paths as you. Fill your mind with

writings by authors who can "pump you up." Some authors may be ministers who offer hope and healing to the broken hearted, and some may be other authors who have been successful and who have made godly principles part of their daily lives—they are people who don't listen to those who tell them they *can't* do something. We are living in times when we must rise above the negative voices that shout," No hope," or "It can't be done." What did Jesus say? "And looking at them Jesus said to them, 'With people this is impossible, but with God all things are possible'" (Matt.19:26 NASB).

Let's rise above the negative voices in order to become a positive voice in the world—a voice that can offer others a better way of living by sharing the message of Jesus.

Life isn't hopeless. You can be healed from your wounds and your past. You can be successful. You can rise above the chaos and negativity if you trust Jesus with your life and your future. Proverbs 23 says, "Surely there is a future, / And your hope will not be cut off" (v. 18 NASB).

Have you felt beaten down by the world's voices? Have others left you feeling depressed or anxious? Take it to Jesus. Ask Him to set you on a new path. You can be set free to become the person God intends you to be.

Let's get pumped up for Jesus and cause a ruckus! Let's rise above the noise and make some loud, positive noises of our own.

5

Walls that Bind

*"I am come that they might have life, and that they might have it
more abundantly" —John 10:10.*

Emptiness. Anger. Hate. Intolerance. Envy. Jealousy.
Resentment. Depression. Feelings of worthlessness. A
broken heart.

Everyone has felt these emotions at one time or another.
I've had good times and bad times. Some days shine bright,
and some days the storm clouds roll in. And so goes the
circle of life.

When life begins to take a nosedive, something causes it.
When did your life take a turn for the worse? Hopefully,

you'll be able to peel back some of layers and find the *root* cause to your dilemma.

When I look back over my life, I discover that sometimes my greatest obstacle is *me*. And sometimes not. But when we decide to let go of the past, which isn't always easy, then we can start working toward changing our future.

Do You Feel that Your Life Is Broken?

Have you lost hope in your current situation? Do hours turn into days, days into months, and months into years without much change? Does your lack of enthusiasm flow like a river through your days, leaving you feeling hopeless? I've been there. We all have.

If this is where you are, take a step back, breathe deeply, and put on a fresh set of lenses. Change your thinking, and get a new perspective on your life. One step at a time. Maybe no one can change your situation, but there are people around you who care. I care. Maybe you're not aware of who they are. Maybe you have never met them, but maybe they are silently praying for you.

What I'm Not . . .

I'm no scholar, no college professor. I have no doctoral degree, and I'm not an ordained minister. I don't pretend to be any of these. What I do have is the experience of knowing what it's like to go through trials. And trials help to strengthen us so that we can be a vessel for God in helping others. James said, "Consider it all joy, my brethren, when you encounter various trials, knowing that the testing of your faith produces endurance. And let endurance have its perfect result, so that you may be perfect and complete, lacking in nothing (James 1:2-4). We can learn from our mistakes, which can be used as one of the keys to our success.

Sometimes unexpected things happen. Sometimes we get kicked around and get our hearts trampled by someone's thoughtless words or deeds. Some people can be so disrespectful that we stand in awe of the situation.

I'm currently working on a political drama/mystery. In this story, as political and social darkness cover the land, one of my main characters discovers that a darkness has clouded her relationship with God, which affects her relationship with her career, her family and others. How she chooses to deal with her problems shows her true character. And how we choose to deal with our circumstances reveals our true character.

Relationships matter. Family matters. God matters.

We are here for a purpose, and everyone's purpose is different and unique. We're all in this together, and we need God first and foremost if we're going to walk through life successfully in a healthy way. We also need our families, as well as friends who are willing to love us enough to walk alongside us without judging, to help us up when we fall and to be the first ones to lift us up with encouragement and prayers. We also need to be there for them when they are struggling.

Life's circumstances can either break us or make us better. We should always try to choose the right path that will help us to become our best no matter how others treat us.

If you're facing a difficult situation, you're not alone. If you're suffering, you're not alone. If you feel there's no hope, you're not alone. Don't believe the lie that your situation is hopeless.

Hope for a Hurting Heart

The world offers false hope . . . a false sense of security. God offers us genuine hope. He helps us tear down walls instead of build them. Walls keep people trapped, and bricks build walls. You're familiar with the names on the bricks. Emptiness. Anger. Hate. Intolerance. Envy. Jealousy. Resentment. Depression. Feelings of worthlessness. A broken heart. All of these result in a hurting heart.

Life is a journey. We can be healed from our past. We can live abundant lives, but we have to want to change course. Do we have a desire to live hopeful lives that we can be excited about? What kind of a life do you envision would bring you joy and satisfaction?

I used to believe that an abundant life was for everyone but me. But this was the lie I believed. Jesus said, "I am come that they might have life, and that they might have it more abundantly" (John 10:10). An abundant life is for everyone who puts his or her trust in Christ.

Are you ready to begin your journey? Are you ready to change what hasn't been working in your life? If so, take out a clean canvas and *begin painting a new beginning*. Your journey will begin when you discover your purpose.

The next chapter will explain why it's important to stay positive and rise above the negative noise of the world in order to make a difference not only in our lives, but in the lives of others.

6
Sheep among Wolves

"I am the good Shepherd; the good shepherd lays down His life for the sheep."—John 10:11 NASB

A blanket of darkness covers our land, smothering America.

Social media is a big contributor because it has hijacked our thoughts, feelings, and actions. The darkness has been growing and simmering for years. Our lives have become entrenched beneath a cloud of darkness, and the light has become obscured.

Have you ever wondered how we got to this point? Here is what I believe has been happening. Let's go beyond politics and all the noise and realize that there are wolves in the world, and there are sheep. Wolves are social animals that travel in packs, and each pack has a leader called the *alpha male*. They are nocturnal; they sleep in the day and roam at night seeking their prey. They are carnivores: they eat only meat. They are stronger in numbers but are cautious creatures. Wolves assess their situation before leaping into action.

To make an analogy, *human wolves* roam our country, too, disguised as social media, politicians, college professors, and teachers. I include college professors and teachers only because some are mixing their social agendas with the basics of learning: *reading, writing, and arithmetic. Some are even changing America's history.* (For those professors and teachers who are not, I applaud you.) They seek to attack the sheep—chew us up and spit us out, if you will. They prey on sheep who are sick and weak. Those who haven't the strength to fight will pay a heavy price in the end.

Like real wolves, human wolves are scavengers—animals or organisms that feed on dead organic matter—and they don't stay in one place too long. They're known to travel up to twelve miles a day; but in this case, they can travel the world in the blink of an eye through our modern means of communication. They communicate by howling, barking, growling, whining, and disrupting the calm.

The Need for a Shepherd

On the tender side of the animal kingdom are the sheep. Sheep must rely heavily on their master—the Good Shepherd—to take care of them. Some may think this is a sign of weakness when in fact it's their greatest strength, because "I can do all things through Him who strengthens me" (Phil 1:13 NASB). A shepherd works hard to protect his sheep because he knows the dangers that lurk.

Sheep need endless attention and the utmost care. Their masters must keep a vigilant watch. Because of the disproportionate weight of their bodies, they can fall down, roll over, making it impossible for them to get up without the help of their shepherd. They will flail, bleat, and fight to right themselves, but if their master doesn't rescue them in time, gas collects in their four-compartment stomach, eventually suffocating them. This is the description of *cast down* sheep. King David knew how it felt to be cast down (Ps. 42:11 NASB). Some shepherds go to great lengths to provide their flock with the best of everything: plentiful grazing, green pastures, unlimited water sources, keeping pests away, and so on. Just like Jesus does His own.

There are other managers who do little to care for their flock because all these managers care about is the fleece (profits); and as a result, the flock suffers and flounders *among the thorns.* When a shepherd neglects his sheep, and doesn't keep a vigilant watch, the sheep are subject to falling prey to wolves, dogs, cougars, or rustlers. Sheep are at the mercy of their keepers.

We are like sheep. We are easily distracted, and we can become unaware of what is going on around us as we rifle through life on a daily basis. We live in our own little pastures, feeling safe and secure in a ravenous world as we graze on the green richness of God's blessings. But there are wolves prowling around and trying to find a way in to attack.

These wolves are not just at our back doors or looking through our fences, they've broken down the gates to our communities and are roaming free, seeking those whom they can devour. They are our true enemies, and we are their prey. They have crossed the line, and they are filled with fury and rage because they are hungry for souls. They won't stop until they devour us. Their mission is to seek and *destroy*. While the sheep have been asleep, the wolves have crept in and pillaged our cities, towns, and villages. It is time for the timid sheep to wake up, open our sleepy eyes, and realize that the wolves can no longer be ignored. They must be driven out of our towns.

Where Do the Wolves Get Their Appetite?

Hate. Hate kills. Hate lies. Hate slanders. Hate harms. Hate destroys. Hate corrupts. Hate resents. Hate causes public discourse. And hate hates. It hates law and order. It hates anyone who disagrees with it. And most of all, it hates Christians, God, Jesus, and Christianity.

Hate Hates Everything Good and Righteous

Human wolves hate because they have an appetite for power and control. That hate bursts forth from hearts of a dark reservoir that have already been stolen by other wolves because they didn't have the Good Shepherd. They weren't strong enough to fight, and therefore, they were overtaken by the enemy.

Hate devours those who stand in its way. It overtakes unsuspecting souls as it conquers its prey. Hate will pounce, attack, and kill. And our enemies' hatred for us can never be quenched until the love of Jesus Christ enters their hearts.

Hate's prey is those who are not paying attention to the world around them. *The unsuspecting bystanders.*

As I said earlier, I've always believed that if we don't get to the *root* of a problem, then we'll be overtaken by it because it's the root that provides strength. A tree's roots must be strong if the tree is to survive. When we discover the root of any one of our problems, and address it, then we can be better able to solve the problem. Jesus will help!

I'm reminded in Psalm 23 that Jesus is our Shepherd. David knew well who his Shepherd was, and he depended on God for strength and courage to go through "the valley of the shadow of death" (v. 4). We must do the same.

Are there wolves prowling about your life waiting to pounce?

How Do We Overcome?

Wolves prey on the weak. We can overcome by accepting Christ as our personal Savior. Staying in God's Word. By praying. By talking with other Christians. And by being around those who love and care for us the way Christ loves and cares for His church. We must not give the wolves the opportunity to wreak havoc in our lives. What should you do if there are others who bring you down more than lift you up? Keep your distance until you're strong enough to be around them.

It is my pray that we can stand strong with the sword and shield that our Lord provides and keep the wolves at bay. God's grace will help us if we lean on the Good Shepherd.

7

What's Missing from Your Life?

The Light shines in the darkness, and the darkness did not comprehend it—John 1:5 NASB

As we look around at the state of affairs in our country, we see violence, protests, chaos, strife and unrest; but if we look past these actions, we can see that these things are only symptoms of hurting hearts, inward strife, and broken lives of people who have lost hope. Skin color makes no difference because a heart is a heart, and what comes forth from our hearts is either love or hate "for his mouth speaks from that which fills his heart" (Luke 6:45 NASB). So race is not an issue here.

My heart breaks when I hear violent speech and see violent actions, especially from movie stars and politicians, because their actions come from seeds of hate, and they are planting those seeds in the lives of others. Possibly their hate stems from disappointed and broken lives—maybe bad childhoods—and they may have never been shown real love. Or maybe their lives have been a cycle of abuses and disappointments. They're angry, so they hate. And they hate because they're angry. But I believe that if we were to delve deeper into their lives, the persons they really hate are themselves.

I find it the most heartbreaking that hate not only trickles down from generation to generation, but it seems to be gushing onto the youth of today. For some, hate becomes a way of life when it's allowed to grow and fester. It seeps into society and poisons the unsuspecting and endangers everyone around it.

David cried out to God in Psalm 25: "The troubles of my heart are enlarged; / Bring me out of my distresses" (v. 17 NASB). Do people who live in strife today call out to God? Has anyone ever shown them "a more excellent way"? (1 Cor. 12:31). Maybe. Hopefully.

Everyone Has a Story

Whether we like it or not, our past shapes who we become—good or bad—and, like it or not, it's part of life's process of growth. But we do have a choice as to how we *want* our past to shape us. Without God's intervention, we are doomed to become prisoners of our past without a way of escape sometimes harboring resentment.

The apostle John said, "The Light shines in the darkness, and the darkness did not comprehend it" (John 1:5 NASB). Before a person accepts Jesus as his or her personal Savior, the person lives in a world of darkness—in sin. Sin separates us from God. Seeing the *Light of Life* (Jesus) becomes difficult through the lens of darkness, but not impossible.

When we witness the state of our society, we know that the world needs Jesus. But many people in the world don't realize they need Him, or they don't want to admit it because they *want* to reject Him. Some will say they are atheists, which is hard for me to comprehend, because it's hard for me to imagine living in a world without the presence of God and Jesus. And wouldn't this mean that there would be no good in the world?

But when people turn their faces to the light of Jesus, things change . . . lives change, and a whole new world opens. How can people know what it's like to live for God— to serve a living God—when all they have ever known was to reject Him? How can they possibly know what living for God is like if they've never experienced Him on a personal level?

So I ask: Do those who are entangled in the things of this world really know what they're missing when they reject Jesus Christ as their personal Savior? Do you? How can you know the joy that comes from living for Jesus if you've never experienced Him? How can you know what it's like to have a loving God wash you clean of your past sins in the blood of Christ's forgiveness and grace if you've never accepted Him as your personal Savior?

Jesus is the only One who can cleanse the world from hate.

I mentioned earlier that I am working on a new book. In the book, the main character has drifted from God's principles since she got elected to the House of Representatives. But when things go from bad to worse after uncovering a horrific secret her world turns upside down.

Your life, too, may turn in an unfavorable direction, and you may have obstacles to overcome. We all experience tough times, and they come and go. But when the rubber truly meets the road, to whom do you run? Lean on? Find strength in?

The world is the wrong place to turn. By putting your faith and trust in worldly relationships, you will surely be tossed about as though on the open seas of life without a raft. Wouldn't you rather turn to the only One who has the power to save and protect you?

God and His Son, Jesus, shines a light on a dark world. Hurting hearts are desperate for the kind of love that only Christ can offer, but many don't realize what they're missing. Many will turn their backs and walk away, never knowing what it's really like to trust in a Savior, to find comfort in times of trouble, or to experience His blessings because they have too much pride to submit their lives to Christ. "Pride goeth before destruction, and an haughty spirit before a fall" (Pr 16:18 NASB).

It's important to plant seeds. Jesus said, "I am the way, and the truth, and the life; no one comes to the Father but through Me" (Jn 14:6 NASB).

Remember: hurting hearts will:

Lash out

Abuse

Hurt

Destroy

We need to stop the cycle. Let's reach out and try to understand the underlying cause for seeds of hate.

Hurting hearts need Jesus.

8
What's In a Name?

A good name is rather to be chosen than great riches—Proverbs 22:1
NASB

When I was growing up, I remember my dad telling us kids, "Be careful how you act and what you say because your name will follow you."

I had two older brothers, each of us five years apart. As I followed my brother who was closest to my age through school, I met many of this teachers and coaches along the way, and I began to notice that he had made a name for himself. Throughout my school years, teachers would ask me if I was his sister. When I said yes, they would tell me what a wonderful guy he was or that they had thought the world of him. As the years passed, my face glowed when they asked me this question. I grew proud to be known as his sister, and therefore, I tried to keep our name spotless.

How do you want your name remembered when someone speaks it? Will people speak favorably or ill about you? Proverbs 22:1 says, "A good name is rather to be chosen than great riches." My dad was right.

The Fruit We Bear

Thanksgiving and Christmas are the two times of the year when we normally stop to reflect and thank God for what we have been given. We pray for health, safety, spiritual well-being, knowledge, wisdom, and understanding; and some pray for wealth. But do we pray that the fruit of Spirit will become more prevalent in our lives toward others? I know sometimes we can speak a pretty good *game*, try to say all the *right things*, and do our best to *sell* Jesus to others, but how do we walk in His sight? Do we lie, cheat, and steal?

For those of us who are Christians, can we walk down the street, figuratively speaking, knowing that others can tell we're followers of Jesus? Can others see that we love Him with our heart, strength, mind, and soul by the way we treat others?

Have you struggled with this? For whatever reason, our

tongues get in the way; we say things we shouldn't or remain silent when we should say something. Sometimes we get frustrated, and before we know it we're acting unchristian. It can be frustrating. "Why did I do that?" "Why did I say that?" And on and on. I'm sure we've all been there, and it's good that we feel bad about it because that means it bothers us enough to be more aware of it.

However, if this behavior becomes a pattern, it's something that we need to address; because good or bad, our names will follow us, and we'll be thought of as a *not-so-friendly soul*. And although we're covered by God's grace, we don't want to have a bad reputation.

The Name above All Names

More than two thousand years ago in the tiny town of Bethlehem, a Savior was born. An angel of the Lord appeared in a dream to Joseph to proclaim that Mary would bear a Son. The angel said, "You shall call His name Jesus, for He will save His people from their sins" (Matthew 1:21 NASB).

Jesus' name is powerful enough to save us from our sins, "And there is salvation in no one else; for there is no other name under heaven that has been given among men by which we must be saved" (Acts 4:12 NASB).

When we say or think the name of Jesus, it means something, and a wonderful feeling comes over us. Have you ever noticed that just saying the name of Jesus is like a breath of fresh air? It is to me. Our unseen enemies even flee at the mention of His name.

Jesus. Jesus. Jesus.

Yes. That is the name that can save us. There is no other name in heaven or earth that can bring salvation.

Jesus said in Matthew 28, "All authority has been given to Me in heaven and on earth. Go therefore and make disciples of all the nations, baptizing them in the name of the Father and the Son and the Holy Spirit" (vv. 18-20 NASB).

Jesus told His disciples, "Many will come in My name, saying, 'I am He!' and will mislead many," and "You will be hated by all because of My name" (Mark 13:6, 13 NASB).

In Acts 2:38, Peter told the crowd, "Repent, and each of you be baptized in the name of Jesus Christ for the forgiveness of your sins; and you will receive the gift of the Holy Spirit." Three thousand people became Christ-followers that day (v. 41).

For more than two thousand years, Jesus' name has been recognized across the world, and most people know it today. If they don't, they will. It is a name above all names. And for those of us who follow Him, we should strive to make His name famous.

What's In a Name?

A lot. That is why so many have tried to erase Jesus' name from history and the public square. They want all traces of Him and His name to be removed from society. They keep trying, but they will never be able to do it because He is so much more than just a name. They will never erase Him from the hearts and lives of His children because He's real, and He lives. Let's continue to speak His holy name because therein lies our strength.

What kind of name are you making for yourself? It's never too late.

9
Faith: How Do You Get It when You Don't Have It?

So then faith cometh by hearing, and hearing by the word of God"—
Romans 10:17

Years ago, I began thinking about what was most important about the Christian faith. There are too many important things to count; and although grace is vital, there is another vital aspect: *Faith*. The writer of Hebrews said, "Without faith, it is impossible to please him: for he that cometh to God must believe that he is, and that he is a rewarder of them that diligently seek him" (11:6).

Faith, Not Sight

As children, my siblings and I trusted our parents to protect us and keep us safe. It's a natural-born instinct to trust our parents and those in authority (unless they have proved themselves to be untrustworthy) because it is the way we've been created.

Olivia grew up with adoptive parents. When she became an adolescent she began wondering about her life. She had more questions than answers. How did she know there was a Jesus? How did she know who created the world? And how could she know what lay beyond our world in an infinite universe when her eyes could not see beyond the physical? How could she even know that she had biological parents when she had been adopted? *And this is the question: How can anyone believe in something their eyes can't see?*

Olivia wanted to believe these things were real. She *needed* to believe them. She needed to believe that Someone had created her (and the universe) and that she had biological parents. She wondered how some people had faith to believe in things they couldn't see and others didn't.

Off to the library she went, in search of some books on the topic of faith. Although there were many it seemed some had their own definitions of the word. She walked away confused, and her question still remained: "How do I get faith when I have little to none?"

Before leaving the library, she scanned the spines of some books and found a title that caught her attention in another section of the library. It had nothing to do with faith, but rather adoption. It was titled, *When You've Been Adopted.* Curious, Olivia slipped the book off the shelf and found a quiet corner.

As she began reading, she had an eye-opening experience. Since she knew she had been adopted, she knew she had to have biological parents even though she'd never met them.

How did she know? Instinct? Maybe. Faith? Yes.

We are all born with a natural instinct to believe that God indeed exists, no matter what anyone has to say about it. Just because someone doesn't *believe* God exists doesn't mean that He doesn't. We can't base truth on our feelings or our own beliefs that don't agree with God's Word. It's possible to talk ourselves into not believing God is real, but is that a reliable conclusion? Some persons believe there are no absolute truths; but does that mean they don't exist, even if you base it solely on what you think is true? Truth doesn't depend on our feelings or our emotions or what we might believe. Truth depends on God's Word.

You see, Olivia had never met her parents, yet she knew she had biological parents. How could she know for sure that she had biological parents? She believed. *Faith.* "Faith is the substance of things hoped for, the evidence of things not seen" (Heb.11:1).

Olivia began to understand that *she* was the "evidence" of something she'd not seen: her birth parents. She knew she had birth parents because they were the (unseen) evidence of her existence. She was the product of their union; therefore, she knew *they* existed because *she* existed.

This opened Olivia's understanding of real faith. She understood that the truth of her existence didn't depend on whether someone could *see* her, but the truth depended on the *evidence* that she existed.

It's the same with our Creator. We have been created by Someone—God—even though we cannot see Him, because we are the evidence—the product—of His existence.

Truth isn't dependent upon what we *"think"* is true; but rather, our faith is dependent upon the unseen truths that we know to be evident. This is called *blind faith*: believing in something when you can't see it and basing our faith on the evidence that exists.

A Journey of Faith

Just as Olivia struggled with faith, I struggled with having the faith to believe that God's grace was for me too. That period in my life caused me to realize that no one could save me from my dilemma but God—that's grace. No one can forgive sins but Jesus. Man hasn't been given the authority to forgive man's sins spiritually speaking. Only Jesus. I was forced to become dependent on His mercy, forgiveness, and grace. I realized that He loved me so much, and because of His love I was free to live in Christ without fear.

I told you how Olivia's faith began. This is how the seed of my faith first began:

I was around ten years old. My best friend at that time was my little dog, Susie. She was my world. She was the smartest dog I ever knew. She did tricks; she talked to us by howling whenever we gave her a cue; she danced on two feet; she had a different bark for humans and another bark for animals; and she was a great watchdog even though she wasn't real big. We could even let her outside with no worries about her running off because she would never leave our yard, *ever*. I loved her with all my heart, and she lived to be twenty-one years old!

But one warm, summer day, I let her outside. I was home alone, and I realized that she had been outside a little longer than usual, so I went out and hunted and called for her as I circled the house several times. This went on for about fifteen to twenty minutes. She was simply gone. Disappeared into thin air!

I can't express how sick I felt. Downtrodden would be a better word. I went back inside hoping for a miracle. I ran to my bedroom and did what any ten-year-old girl would do when she realizes she's lost her best friend; I lay in bed and sobbed for a good long time while I prayed feverishly and asked God to bring her back.

Finally, with blurry eyes, I trudged back into the living room. I wiped my eyes, and when I looked out our big picture window, right there, standing beneath our big tree, was my little Susie sniffing the ground as if nothing had happened. I can't explain the joy that filled my soul, and I couldn't stop thanking God for bringing my dog back to me. To this day, I have no idea where she was or why she didn't come when I called, but God was watching, and He saw my tears, He heard the plea of a little girl and brought my dog back.

This was how the seed of my faith in God first began, and it's been growing ever since. God works in ways that we can't understand. He meets us where we are.

Growing Your Faith through Scripture Reading

Sometimes real faith in God and Jesus comes the way it did for me, but there is one sure way it happens: "So then faith cometh by hearing, and hearing by the word of God" (Rom.10:17).

John's Gospel tells us, "But these are written, that ye might believe that Jesus is the Christ, the Son of God; and that believing ye might have life through his name (20:31).

God's Word is the perfect place to begin your faith journey and establish a firm foundation of faith that cannot be shaken. Sometimes people wait for their emotions to lead them to some sort of big awakening. There's nothing wrong with emotions; God created us with emotions, but faith isn't based on emotions. Emotions can change. God's Word never changes.

We must always check our emotions against God's Word. We need the firm foundation of faith that will hold beyond our emotions. Have you ever heard someone say, "I don't *feel* saved," or "I'm saved because I can *feel* it"? Feelings shouldn't be the litmus test for salvation and faith, but rather, the promises contained in God's Word.

As we develop the habit of reading and studying the Bible, we begin to develop a deeper understanding of things as our faith in Him grows. We realize that we're not always going to be happy, sad, depressed, or exuberant because our emotions come and go. This is human nature.

Seeds of faith are planted, watered, and grow within our

hearts because they are nurtured by the seeds of His Word; they become a testament to His truths.

If we truly seek Jesus, God will guide us to His Son through Scripture. To those who don't read the Bible, He can use other circumstances to draw us to Him and His Word. But the gospel of John was written to convince humans that Jesus became flesh. John began with "In the beginning was the Word, and the Word was with God, and the Word was God. He was in the beginning with God. All things came into being through Him, and apart from Him nothing came into being that has come into being. In Him was life, and the life was the Light of men. The light shines in the darkness; and the darkness did not comprehend it" (1:1-5 NASB).

Peter also said, "Whom having not seen, ye love; in whom, though now ye see him not, yet believing, ye rejoice with joy unspeakable and full of glory: Receiving the end of your faith, even the salvation of your souls" (1Pet.1:8-9).

God speaks through His Word. He reveals His will through His Word. He reveals who Jesus is through His Word. "Draw nigh to God, and he will draw nigh to you" (James 4:8). Even though God speaks to us through His Word, this is not the only way our faith grows. He works through other Christians, too, to help us along our path to faith.

We, as Christians, have a responsibility to teach others how to obtain faith in God so they can know that absolute truth exists—something desperately lacking in today's society. If not us, then who will go before them and show them the way? If we do not teach the next generation God's truths, or encourage those who are not strong in their faith, "that [their] faith should not stand in the wisdom of men, but in the power of God" (1 Cor. 2:5), they may get swept up by false doctrines and the lies that society teaches them.

Do you know someone struggling to wholeheartedly put his or her faith in Christ? Pray for that person. Offer hope, and "let your speech be always with grace, seasoned with salt, that ye may know how ye ought to answer every man" (Col. 4:6).

10

The Joy of a Child

"Do not be grieved, for the joy of the LORD is your strength." —
Nehemiah 8:10

If you are a Christian, do you remember when you first became one? When you first believed? Remember how you felt? I'm sure you were filled with joy and happy to be a child of the King.

Then years passed; struggles came and went, and came and went again, and the bright light that lit your world maybe faded.

As I sat in church services one day, I noticed something that caused my heart to almost leap within me. A little girl, who was probably eight years old or so, asked her grandmother if she and her sister could sit by themselves a few rows up. The grandmother replied, "Yes, but behave."

Before the message, the pastor asked all the children to come down front to retrieve a sucker. (He uses this time for a quick teaching opportunity.) When the sisters returned to their seats, the one little girl gave her sucker to a senior woman and then gave the woman a hug.

The girl appeared excited, overflowing with joy. During the song service, she became so excited that she put her hand in the air, waved it, and had a smile that stretched from ear to ear. There was no mistake; she was singing "unto the Lord," and that gave me a joyful heart.

We continued singing as the little girl sang and swayed to the music, clapping her hands and smiling. She was truly excited to be in the presence of Jesus; she could hardly contain her excitement, and she didn't even try. My heart swelled to see such joy coming from a child.

When the song service concluded, I felt I had to say something to her. I told her that she was such a bundle of love. I also told her I hoped she would never change and to always keep her eyes on Jesus.

She smiled and nodded and gave me a hug.

Before the service ended, she motioned for me. She said,

"You're my new church buddy." I thanked her and told her how happy I was to be her church buddy, and she gave me another hug.

When I left services that day, my heart was full; not just because of the message, which was inspiring, but also because of a little girl who was full of God's love and joy.

Luke 18 says, "But Jesus called for them, saying, 'Permit the children to come to Me, and do not hinder them, for the kingdom of God belongs to such as these. Truly I say to you, whoever does not receive the kingdom of God like a child will not enter it at all'" (vv. 16-17 NASB).

Jesus loves when we get excited for Him. When children are in church, they don't dwell on what kind of week they had. They seem to be *in the moment* of worship with their hearts and minds on Jesus.

I remember attending Sunday school as a child, and I loved learning about Jesus and the different Bible stories. When I grew up and gave my heart and life to Him, I was anxious to spread the word to anyone who would listen, even to those who didn't really want to hear it. When people give their lives to Jesus, joy really does flood their souls because they know they've received a new, fresh start.

As years go by, however, we can hit some pretty big bumps in the road, which can cause us to lose our joy. But

I'm convinced that living for Christ is a trillion times better than facing life without Him. He is our safety net. "For he will give his angels charge over thee, to keep thee in all thy ways" (Psalm 91:11).

Without Him There Is No Hope

Without Jesus there is no hope, no matter how hard someone searches for it. I have faced some dark days in my life, but I have found that when I've passed through the storm I am stronger and a little wiser. Proverbs 18:10 says, "The name of the LORD is a strong tower: the righteous runneth into it, and is safe."

As humans, we make choices that affect our lives, whether good or bad. And God has given us free will. We're not robots. We're human beings with the freedom to choose. But through the ups and downs, God promises to those who belong to Him, "I will never leave thee nor forsake thee" (Heb.13:5). The fact that He is always with us should bring us joy.

Living for Him

God has given so many promises to those who love Him and endure to the end—to those who have given their lives to Him. Here are just a few:

- Blessed are those who wash their robes, so that they may have the right to the tree of life, and may enter by the gates into the city. (Rev.22:14 NASB)

- Who is the one who overcomes the world, but he who believes that Jesus is the Son of God? (1 John 5:5NASB)

- He who overcomes, I will grant to him to sit down with Me on My throne, as I also overcame and sat down with My Father on His throne." (Rev. 3:21 NASB)

- But as it is written, "Eye hath not seen, nor ear heard, neither have entered into the heart of man, the things which God hath prepared for them that love him." (1Cor. 2:9)

The things we endure in this life will seem inconsequential, compared to what God has in store for those who love Him. Every struggle, every valley, every tear will be worth it when our feet touch those streets of gold, and God's light shines on us. We will experience joy in a new way! Can you imagine running into the arms of Jesus on your first day in heaven?

God gives us the strength to endure life. If ever you feel like giving up, just remember that the road behind you is darker than the road ahead.

May you find childlike joy as God touches your life in a special way.

11

Inside Out

"For God sees not as man sees, for man looks at the outward appearance, but the LORD looks at the heart." —1 Samuel 16:7 NASB

I have to admit that I've put a lot of emphasis on my outward appearance over the years. If I looked good, then I felt good. I would venture to guess you've probably felt the same at one time or another. I think we all want to stay young-looking for as long as we can.

But, as we know, time passes, a little line appears here, a little line there; crow's feet; laugh lines; and kiss lines around the mouth. Next comes the gray hair, and *voila!* You're on your way to another stage of your life.

For us women, maybe some of us have tried all the latest wrinkle creams, serums, Retinol refining night creams, collagen creams, hydroxy acid creams, microdermabrasion, acid peels; and if all else fails, plastic surgery, which this is one step I don't care to take.

We've read the headlines promoting wrinkle-free results if we use their products. We don't really even need to spend time researching to discover that these companies are making billions of dollars on gullible woman who don't want to look as though they're growing old.

It took me about ten years to come to terms with the fact that I am not getting any younger, and if a person lives long enough he or she will eventually grow old and look old. The mystery to me, however, is that of all the places on the body, why do most wrinkles show up on the face?

Some people accept the aging process with grace while others fight it tirelessly. They give up when they realize that all the wrinkle creams in the world won't erase wrinkles. And with all the chemicals in them, I believe they may cause more damage than good. Can they really be good for your face the way the manufacturers say? I don't think so.

Companies spend millions of dollars trying to make you believe that you'll become wrinkle-free in a certain amount of time. After all, the majority of their models are young and beautiful with flawless skin that I'm sure has been airbrushed to *prove* that their products work. My skin looked like that, too, when I was young.

What message is the beauty industry sending to our younger generation of women when they put a great deal of emphasis on outward beauty instead of where it belongs: on inward beauty? I'm sorry to admit, I fell prey to this world of outward beauty promotion myself.

Therefore, as you've probably guessed, my point is this: We know we're not going to live forever. We know we're not going to look young forever. If we live long enough we're going to look older as we age. Proverbs 20:29 says that gray hair is beautiful. "The glory of young men is their strength: /and the beauty of old men is the grey head." So this is good news!

What Is True Beauty?

Sadly, I heard a story once about a mother who sent her daughter to a camp for aspiring models because she wanted her daughter to be perfect and have a chance at a modeling career. But when the daughter returned, she was bulimic (binge-purge syndrome). It was discovered on the show that the girl wanted to be "perfect" *for her mom.* Society has sent young girls down a path for the sake of industry profits, and parents are doing it for fame and fortune. It's troubling.

But God does not pay attention to the outward beauty; He sees the heart, the central core of our being, and this is what parents should teach their daughters. "But the LORD said to Samuel, 'Do not look at his appearance or at the height of his stature, because I have rejected him; for God sees not as man sees, for man looks at the outward appearance, but the LORD looks at the heart'" (1Sam.16:7 NASB).

Proverbs 31 says: "Charm is deceitful and beauty is vain, / But a woman who fears the LORD, she shall be praised" (v. 30 NASB). A person whose outward appearance may be unattractive will become attractive if her beauty comes from within. The right heart and fear of, or respect for, God will bring out the beauty that lies within us.

The Depths of the Heart

Proverbs 23:7 says, "For as he thinketh in his heart, so is he." There have been times when I was glad God knew the intentions of my heart, especially when I was being accused of something that wasn't true. We should always be "on guard" and protect our hearts from outside influences. "Keep thy heart with all diligence; for out of it are the issues of life"

(Prov.4:23).

Even though no beauty product manufacturer, plastic surgeon, or dermatologist can stop the aging process, nor can any physician cause our inward organs to live forever, our inward beauty can continue to show through as long as we grow in Christ. Our physical bodies die daily and will return to dust someday; but our hearts won't wrinkle, they won't shrivel up, and they won't be damaged due to overexposure to sun. Just as we are conscious of our outward appearance, we should be careful to maintain our inward beauty that comes only from a relationship with the Father. This is what we should teach the next generation.

So I leave you with this: " Your adornment must not be merely external—braiding the hair, and wearing gold jewelry, or putting on dresses; but let it be the hidden person of the heart, with the imperishable quality of a gentle and quiet spirit, which is precious in the sight of God" (1 Pet.3:3-4 NASB).

And this: "An excellent wife, who can find? For her worth is far above jewels" (Proverbs 31:10-11 NASB).

"She rises also while it is still night, And gives food to her household, And portions to her maidens" (Proverbs 31:15 NASB).

"She extends her hands to the needy" (Proverbs 31:20

NASB).

"She opens her mouth in wisdom, And the teaching of kindness is on her tongue" (Proverbs 31:26 NASB).

"Charm is deceitful and beauty is vain, But a woman who fears the Lord, she shall be praised" (Proverbs 31:30 NASB)

12

Because He Lives

"For the LORD your God is he that goeth with you, to fight for you against your enemies, to save you"—Deuteronomy 20:4

Enemies. Our enemies. They're all around us, trying to destroy us. Some we can see. Some we can't. Those we can see have faces. Those we can't see lurk in the dark places of society. "For we wrestle not against flesh and blood, but against principalities, against powers, against the rulers of the darkness of this world, against spiritual wickedness in high places" (Eph.6:12). These unseen forces wait for us to stumble, and they hope we take our eyes off Jesus. They are waiting for us to mess up. They don't have faces, but they do have names: *Discouragement. Self-pity. Resentment. Hate.*

Jealousy. Envy. Depression. Suffering. Finger-pointing.

Many of us know these enemies all too well because they are relentless. Their one and only mission: to *seek and destroy*. Our enemies continually try to rid the *marketplace* of Jesus, God's one and only Son. They have tried to destroy our *freedom of religion*. Our enemies believe that once Jesus is taken out of the way, they will have won the battle, and they will be in control at last. Evidently they are not familiar with Isaiah 59:19, "So shall they fear the name of the LORD from the west, and his glory from the rising of the sun. When the enemy shall come in like a flood, the Spirit of the LORD shall lift up a standard against him." How awesome is that!

The Goal of Our Enemies

Nehemiah's enemies tried to prevent the wall around Jerusalem from being rebuilt. They said, "They will not know or see until we come among them, kill them and put a stop to their work." (Neh. 4:11 NASB). Although written a long time ago, this verse demonstrates how our enemies work today.

Enemies of God's people will cause as much havoc as they can, attempting to do whatever is necessary to steal our hope and stop us from doing His work. They want us to believe that they have won the battle before it's even over in an attempt to discourage us. Hope is a strong emotion; but when it has been lost, depression and discouragement fills the gap. Our enemies will stop at nothing to convince us to believe a situation is hopeless. It's one of their main goals.

Think about it. Hopelessness has brought ruin upon many good men and women. Hopelessness sucks the life from our hearts. Hopelessness can destroy and cause people to do things they might never do otherwise. Hopelessness is a thief that wants to steal our souls.

But there is always hope.

No one has the power to steal or destroy our hope unless we allow them to. Why? Because Jesus lives. The song *Because He Lives* by Bill and Gloria Gaither is one of my favorites, and I hold it close to my heart. That song has gotten me through some pretty rough times, and whenever I hear it or sing it, I always know there is hope. I know He lives, and I know I can always face tomorrow. Even now when I sing this song, it fills me with such emotion. Jesus does indeed make life worth living.

The Truth of the Matter

The *world* (those who have not accepted Jesus Christ as their personal Savior) can't know what it's like to walk with the Protector of our souls. Jesus walks behind us to guard our

74

backs, beside us as our Friend, and in front of us to guide us in the right direction, while pushing our enemies aside. How awesome is that? How can the world know what it's like for Someone to pick us up when we fall . . . to carry us when we're not strong enough to walk . . . and to be a light for our path when we're going through dark times in our lives?

I don't believe that society has a *race* problem or a *division* problem or even an *envious of the wealthy* problem. I believe our society has a *heart* problem—hearts filled with hate, resentment, envy, lying tongues, gossiping, and belief in the propaganda that the media grinds out on a daily basis. Precious time wasted.

There is an answer: hope in Jesus the Christ.

What exactly does this mean? It means that those who have accepted Jesus as their personal Savior know that real hope doesn't end on earth. This world doesn't own hope. Heaven owns hope, and because the final destination for the believer is heaven to spend eternity with Jesus, the story of hope continues after death. This is the reason there will always be hope even though we may all experience hopelessness. But there is always hope in Jesus.

So we can face the future because Jesus is alive. Because of Him we have the good news of salvation to share.

The most wonderful part is that this hope is for *everyone*

who accepts Jesus as Savior. It is my prayer that the world would come to know Jesus. It is my prayer that we as Christ-followers will not be ashamed of the gospel of Jesus Christ, "for it is the power of God for salvation to everyone who believes, to the Jew first and also to the Greek. For in it the righteousness of God is revealed from faith to faith; as it is written, 'But the righteous man shall live by faith'" (Rom.1:16-17 NASB).

Our enemies have no chance against us, and we can play a part to help change hearts and lives by guiding people toward Jesus.

I close this chapter with some of my favorite verses in the Bible:

> Wherefore take unto you the whole armor of
> God, that ye may be able to withstand in the
> evil day, and having done all, to stand. Stand
> therefore, having your loins girt about with
> truth, and having on the breastplate of
> righteousness; And your feet shod with the
> preparation of the gospel of peace; Above all,
> taking the shield of faith, wherewith ye shall
> be able to quench all the fiery darts of the
> wicked. And take the helmet of salvation, and
> the sword of the Spirit, which is the word of

God: Praying always with all prayer and supplication in the Spirit, and watching there unto with all perseverance and supplication for all saints; And for me [the Apostle Paul], that utterance may be given unto me, that I may open my mouth boldly, to make known the mystery of the gospel. (Eph.6:13-19)

13

Grace

For by grace you have been saved through faith; and that not of yourselves, it is the gift of God. — Ephesians 2:8

I'd like to end this book as it began and with what I believe to be one of the most uplifting words in the biblical text— one of many gifts that God can bestow on us—*Grace*. There is so much more to this word, and I can only touch on it here.

Grace is something we don't deserve. We can't work for it; we can't earn it; we can't pay for it. It's a gift from God that He so lovingly decided to give sinners, because He realized that humans couldn't live up to the high expectations laid out for humanity in the Old Testament. The Old

Testament is great, and we can learn so much from it. But when Jesus died on the cross, He left us a New Covenant... The New Testament. There were many dos and don'ts in the Old Testament that were not easy to live by, but God provided us with another way. He sent His Son, Jesus, to earth because of His great love for us. He extended mercy so that we could live abundant lives and be free "from the law of sin and death" (Rom. 8:2.) The Old Testament was *the law*. The New Testament is *grace*.

Living without God's presence can be scary because life can feel empty and full of darkness with no hope of better things to come. When troubles and trials do come, we can sometimes feel that there is no one who can help. We don't want to go through hard times, but sometimes we feel that we don't have a choice. It seems as if we are living a nightmare, and we hope we'll wake up and be on our joyful way. Sometimes, though, we sink deeper into despair.

Like the book I read so long ago, *The Wall*, we search for a way out until it seems we can't go one step farther. Our hearts ache as the thorns from our trials grow, with each step on the path seeming worse than the one before it. If only we could feel safe again. When we look back, the road behind us is darker than the road ahead, and that's when we realize that we must keep going if we're going to make it. As hope vanishes, the sky grows darker, the pain grows stronger.

We have many questions: Why am I going through this? Why are these things happening to me? As we stumble along, one unbearable step after the next, we pray that the path we are traveling will lead us toward the light. We fight to survive, searching for not only a way out of our circumstances but for something that will give us direction and purpose. When we finally run out of strength, we fall, overcome from exhaustion.

Then something happens inside of us that urges us to keep going and not give up—we regain the will to survive because our Father loves us. We feel something warm as we lift our heads. We see a small, flickering light that offers a bit of hope. We feel a presence, even though we see no one. And that presence is God. He is there to extend His grace.

God will speak to our hearts silently and tenderly when we are ready to receive His words. What have we done that God would extend His grace to us? *Nothing.* "For by grace you have been saved through faith; *and that not of yourselves, it is the gift of God*" (Eph. 2:8, italics mine).

Then it hits us. We rise and stand with a renewed hope. Once-withered limbs now surge with energy. The glimmer of light that we had seen has now spread fully and is warming our faces. The sky clears, and there's a new song in our hearts that affirms we are going in the right direction. We step swiftly toward the light of Jesus. We have faith to realize that God was there all along and that He loves and cares for us.

We can emerge victorious if we put our trust in Him. God reaches down from heaven because of His infinite love, mercy, forgiveness, and . . . *grace*. He reaches down, lifts us up, and gives us the strength to face another day.

Sometimes our days feel like a hard-fought battle or a laborer's weary grind. During the day we desire the coolness of the evening, and through the restless night we long for a peaceful morning. Misery will try to break down the door of our hearts, begging to gain entry, and it will keep coming back as long as we let it in. We must not let it.

God wants us to want Him. He wants us to overcome. He's on our side. He's cheering for us to not give up. He wants us to become rocks that won't crumble under the weight of our enemies, because He knows that the enemy will attack our weakest point to gain entry into our lives and our hearts.

May you forever walk in the fullness, joy, peace, and grace of our Lord and Savior, Jesus Christ.

~Blessings

If you haven't accepted Jesus as your personal Savior, these scriptures will help guide you in the right direction.

Your New Journey Begins...

Understand the need for salvation ~

"For all have sinned, and come short of the glory of God." ~ Romans 3:23

"For the wages of sin is death; but the gift of God is eternal life through Jesus Christ our Lord." ~ Romans 6:23

Hear the Gospel Message ~

"So then faith cometh by hearing, and hearing by the word of God." ~ Romans 10:17

Believe that Jesus is God's Son ~

"For God so loved the world, that He gave His only begotten Son, that whosoever believeth in him should not perish, but have everlasting life." ~ John 3:16

"But without faith it is impossible to please him: for he that cometh to God must believe that he is, and that he is a rewarder of them that diligently seek him." ~ Hebrews 11:6

Repent (turn away from your old life and walk in a new life)

"I tell you, Nay: but, except ye repent, ye shall all likewise perish." ~ Luke 13:3

Confess that Jesus is the Christ; God's Son ~

"That if thou shalt confess with thy mouth the Lord Jesus, and shalt believe in thine heart that God hath raised him from the dead, thou shalt be saved. For with the heart man believeth unto righteousness; and with the mouth confession is made unto salvation." ~ Romans 10:9-10

"Fight the good fight of faith, lay hold on eternal life, whereunto thou art also called, and hast professed a good profession before many witnesses." ~ 1 Timothy 6:12

Be immersed in water baptism ~

"He that believeth and is baptized shall be saved; but he that believeth not shall be damned." ~ Mark 16:16

"Therefore let all the house of Israel know assuredly, that God hath made the same Jesus, whom ye have crucified, both Lord and Christ. Now when they heard this, they were pricked in their heart, and said unto Peter and to the rest of the apostles, Men and brethren, what shall we do? Then Peter said unto them, Repent, and be baptized every one of you in the name of Jesus Christ for the remission of sins, and ye shall receive the gift of the Holy Ghost." ~ Acts 2:36-38

"For as many of you as have been baptized into Christ

have put on Christ." ~ Galatians 3:27

"And they continued steadfastly in the apostles' doctrine and fellowship, and in breaking of bread, and in prayers." ~ Acts 2:42

I pray that you may remain faithful and enjoy your life to its fullest. God cares. He loves you. He wants you to want Him.

Remember to examine the scriptures to see whether the things you're told are true:

"Now these were more noble-minded than those in Thessalonica, for they received the word with great eagerness, examining the Scriptures daily to see whether these things were so." ~ Acts 17:11 (NAS)

About The Author

Debbie's love of writing began at an early age. She has a lifelong desire to encourage others through her writing so they may grow to have a closer relationship with Jesus Christ. She enjoys planting seeds of faith and watching the fruit from God's hands water them. She hopes others will discover their God-given purpose so they can be a positive influence in the world. People need people.

God is the wind beneath her wings, and Jesus is the Rock of her salvation.

Debbie enjoys spending time with family and friends, making gel candles, playing golf, bicycling with her dog, Ringo, along with gardening and other outdoor activities.

Debbie is working on her next work of fiction where her main characters become torn between doing what's right or doing what's easy.

You can sign up for updates on her work at:
https://www.debra-erickson.com/, or
https://www.debra-erickson.com/newsletter or
candidlychristian.com

Debbie's other sites:
heholdsourfuture.wordpress.com
https://daerickson.wordpress.com/
www.pinterest.com/daerickson77/

A Personal Word from Debbie

It is my desire to magnify the name of Jesus so that He will draw all men unto Him. (John 12:32) Society is going down the wrong path and has gone astray. Society is going to great lengths to erase Jesus from the public domain. Therefore, we must strive to keep Him, and His name alive.

As we see the day drawing nearer to the coming of our Lord, let us turn to Him so others may come to know Him by our example.

If this book has inspired you, and you believe it will inspire someone in your life and help them grow their faith, please feel free to pass it on or give it as a gift. We all need some hope and encouragement along our journey.

May you be healed from your pain, and may God bless you richly on your path to discovering His will for your life.

May the Light of Jesus give you comfort, encouragement, strength and hope.